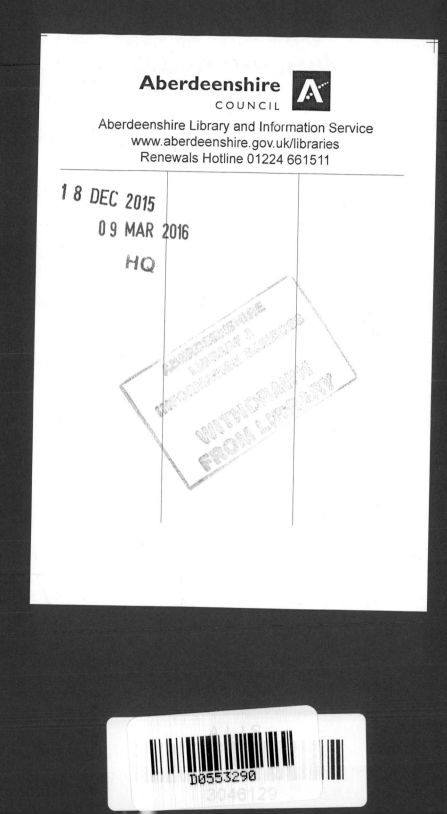

www.raintreepublishers.co.uk
Visit our website to find out more information about Raintree books.

To order:
☎ Phone 0845 6044371
🖷 Fax +44 (0) 1865 312263
🖳 Email myorders@raintreepublishers.co.uk

Customers from outside the UK please telephone +44 1865 312262

Raintree is an imprint of Capstone Global Library Limited, a company incorporated in England and Wales having its registered office at 7 Pilgrim Street, London, EC4V 6LB – Registered company number: 6695582

Text © Capstone Global Library Limited 2011
First published in hardback in 2011
The moral rights of the proprietor have been asserted.

Edited by Megan Cotugno
Designed by Ryan Frieson
Original illustrations © Capstone Global Library, Ltd.
Illustrated by Planman Technologies
Picture research by Mica Brancic
Originated by Capstone Global Library, Ltd.
Printed and bound in China by Leo Paper Products Ltd.

ISBN 978 1 4062 2166 4
15 14 13 12 11
10 9 8 7 6 5 4 3 2 1

British Library Cataloguing in Publication Data

Fay, Gail.
Using money. -- (Understanding money)
1. Money--Juvenile literature. 2. Finance, Personal--Juvenile literature.
I. Title II. Series
332.4-dc22

Acknowledgements

The author and publishers are grateful to the following for permission to reproduce copyright material:

Alamy pp. 24 (© Michael Spence), 29 (© MARK SYKES WEB SITES), 37 (© Mark Richardson), 38 (© Duncan Hale-Sutton); Corbis pp. 11 (© Andy Rain/epa), 12 (© Image Source), 13 (© Auslöse), 15 (© Leah Warkentin), 17 (© DreamPictures/ Pam Ostrow/Blend Images), 19 (© Reg Charity), 22 (© India Picture), 23 (Dustin Steller/Design Pics), 25 (© Marcus Mok/ Asia Images), 26 (© Sullivan), 27 (Jose Luis Pelaez Inc) , 39 (© Michael Janosz/isiphotos.com), 41 (© RICK WILKING/ Reuters); Getty Images pp. 10 (John-Francis Bourke), 33 (Peter Cade), 35 (Bloomberg/Contributor); iStockphoto.com p. 5 (© Todd Szalkowski); Shutterstock pp. 4 (© Tania Zbrodko), 42 (© Olly), 43 (© Ekaterina Naimushina), 20 (© StockLite), 21 (© Photoinnovation), 30 (© WilleeCole)

Cover photograph of crowd in the shopping centre reproduced with permission of Shutterstock (© Dmitrijs Dmitrijevs).

We would like to thank Michael Miller for his invaluable help in the preparation of this book.

Every effort has been made to contact copyright holders of any material reproduced in this book. Any omissions will be rectified in subsequent printings if notice is given to the publisher.

Contents

You can find the answers to the Solve it! questions on page 45.

Some words are shown in bold, **like this**. You can find out what they mean by looking in the glossary on page 46.

When did people start using money?

Before people used money to pay for things, they **bartered**, or traded, to get things they needed. For example, a farmer and a fisherman might decide to barter. They would trade crops and fish, with no money involved.

Ancient money

Around 6000 BC, people started using cows, sheep, and crops as early forms of money. Each region, or area, assigned values to these animals and food items. For example, three bunches of wheat might buy a knife.

Early forms of money, such as sheep, were hard to carry around and could not be saved for later use.

Money from different countries has different names. Several examples are pictured here, including pesos from Mexico, euros from Austria, and shillings from Kenya.

There were problems with these early forms of money. Animals could get ill and crops could become rotten, so they could not be saved and used later. They were also hard to carry around. As a result, around 1850 BC, people started using small metal lumps called ingots as money.

Modern money

Around 640 BC, the government of Lydia, which is part of present-day Turkey, created the first coins made from metals such as gold and silver. The coins were stamped with pictures of gods or goddesses.

Around AD 800, paper money was invented in China. These banknotes had the same value as metal coins, but they were lighter and easier to carry. Instead of carrying around 10 metal coins worth 10p each, a person could carry one paper £1 note.

Today, everyone around the world uses money to pay for things they want and need. Each country has its own **currency** that is made up of different **denominations** of coins and banknotes.

Where do people get money?

Adults receive wages from their jobs or returns (money earned) on their **investments**. This is the money they use. Where do you get money that you can use?

Gifts

Have you ever received cash in a birthday card? Has a grandparent ever sent you a **cheque** as a Christmas present? When you are young, gifts might be one of your main sources of money.

Pocket money

Do you get weekly or monthly pocket money? Do your parents pay you for doing jobs around the house, such as cleaning your room? Every family is different. If your pocket money is small or if you do not get any, do not worry! There are other ways to get your own money.

What can you do with your money?

Save = Put money aside for big expenses or spending later.

Spend = Buy things you need and want.

Invest = Use your money to make more money.

Share = Give money away to help others.

Extra chores

Relatives or neighbours might pay you for doing extra chores. These are usually bigger jobs, such as mowing the grass, washing the car, raking leaves, or cleaning the garage. If your neighbours or relatives do not offer, you can ask if they have jobs you can do.

Selling things

If your family has a garage sale or does a car boot sale, see if you can sell some of your old things. You can sell toys, clothes, or books. You can also sell things that you make, such as bead bracelets or art work.

Solve it!

Jack receives £10 on his birthday, £5 for raking Mrs Smith's yard, and his monthly pocket money of £16. How much money does Jack receive?

If you are willing to work, you can find many ways to earn your own money.

How do banks work?

People use banks to keep their money safe or to borrow money to buy things such as homes and cars. Banks also lend money to people by providing them with **credit cards**.

A bank is also a business, like a restaurant or a cinema. Like any business, banks have to pay the people who work there. Banks also have to pay for things like electricity and internet connection. Most importantly, banks need to make more money than they spend so they can stay in business.

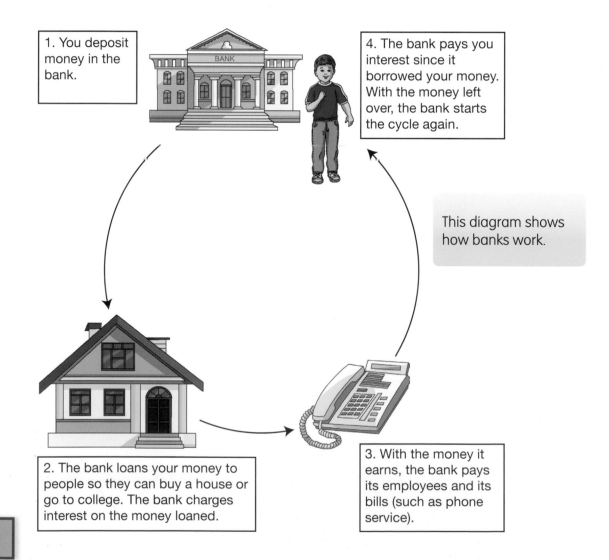

1. You deposit money in the bank.

4. The bank pays you interest since it borrowed your money. With the money left over, the bank starts the cycle again.

This diagram shows how banks work.

2. The bank loans your money to people so they can buy a house or go to college. The bank charges interest on the money loaned.

3. With the money it earns, the bank pays its employees and its bills (such as phone service).

How do banks make money?

When people **deposit**, or put, money in a bank, it does not stay in one place until they come back for it. Banks use their customers' money to bring in **revenue**, or income. Banks make most of their money through **loans**. They lend people money and charge a fee called **interest**. (See the box below to learn how interest is calculated.) The exact percentage a bank charges is called the **interest rate**. As the bank is borrowing its customers' money to make these loans, it pays interest to the customer on the money deposited. The banks make money by charging their loan customers a higher rate of interest than they pay to the depositors who provide the money.

Calculating interest

To work out how much interest is owed, you change the interest rate percentage to a decimal and use the following equation:

amount borrowed x interest rate = interest owed

For example, if someone borrows £10,000 at an annual (yearly) interest rate of 5 per cent, the equation would look like this:

£10,000 x .05 = £500

At the end of the year, this person would owe £10,000, plus £500 in interest.

Can a bank go out of business?

Just like a bookshop or a bakery, a bank can go out of business if it runs out of money and cannot pay its employees or its running costs. With a bank, this can happen if people do not pay back money they have borrowed. The bank loses the money it loaned, as well as the interest.

Between January 2008 and March 2010, over 200 US banks went out of business. They ran out of money after people stopped paying back their loans. Some UK banks and building societies nearly went bankrupt and had to be rescued by the government. The case study on Northern Rock gives an example of what happened.

Banks can go out of business if they don't have many customers.

What happens to your money if a bank goes out of business?

If your bank is **insured** by the **Financial Services Compensation Scheme (FSCS)**, you will probably get all of your money back. The FSCS currently insures money up to £50,000 per person per bank. This means the fund will pay back everything you deposit in each insured bank, up to £250,000 per bank.

Northern Rock

Between 2000 and 2007, Northern Rock made it very easy for people to borrow money to buy a house. The bank offered special loans, called **adjustable-rate mortgages**, which had low interest rates and low monthly payments. Then the interest rate increased, and home owners could not afford the new monthly payments. Thousands of people stopped paying back their loans. Soon, Northern Rock ran out of money. In September 2007, Northern Rock asked the Bank of England, the United Kingdom's central bank, for help.

11

Why is saving important?

Saving money is not easy, but the benefits are worth it. Have you ever borrowed money from your parents or your brother or sister? Then you know what it feels like to be in **debt**, or to owe money. It is not fun! If you borrow from your brother, you might have to give him all your pocket money until you pay him back. It is better to learn the habit of saving. Then you can pay for things on your own even if they come up unexpectedly.

Does saving mean you can never buy treats or go to the cinema? No. It just means you learn to think beyond right now, especially if you are saving for a specific item. Remember that emergencies happen and opportunities come up. If you have been saving money all along and get the chance to go to an amusement park, you are more likely to have enough money to go. If you have been spending all your money, you might have to say no.

Find your own special place to start saving money. For example, you can use a shoebox or a piggy bank.

Age when you start saving	8	8	8
Amount you save each month	£3.00	£5.00	£10.00
TOTAL at age 18 (without interest)	£360.00	£600.00	£1,200.00

Saving a little each month can really add up!

If you are saving for a specific item, such as a remote control car or a puppy, put a picture of what you want on your bedroom wall. Every time you see it you will remember your goal!

A bank can help

Most banks will allow children to open their own **savings account**. Some require a parent's name on the account until you reach a certain age.

There are many reasons to open a savings account at a bank. Firstly, your money cannot get lost or stolen. If you pick a bank that is **FSCS** insured, you will get your money back if the bank goes out of business. Secondly, you are less likely to spend your money if it is out of reach. Finally, your money will grow faster in a savings account because the bank will pay you **interest** in exchange for using your money. The **interest rate** will be a percentage, just like it is on money that is borrowed. Look for a bank that offers **compound interest**, which means you earn money on the **balance** in your account plus the interest already earned.

Age when you start saving	8	8	8
Amount you save each month	£3	£5	£10
Interest rate	5%	5%	5%
TOTAL at age 18	£475.44	£792.41	£1,584.81

Putting your money in a savings account with compound interest can help it grow faster. Compare the totals in this chart with the totals in the chart on page 13.

When you are saving, you need a high interest rate. When you are borrowing, you need a low interest rate.

Helpful hints

Here are some questions to ask before you open a savings account:

① Is this bank FSCS insured?

② Do I have to keep a minimum balance in my account?

③ Do you offer compound interest?

④ What is the interest rate?

⑤ Do you charge fees to open or maintain an account?

If you do not have a savings account, ask your parents to help you open one. You can deposit whatever money you have saved.

What is a current account used for?

Savings accounts are used for setting money aside for later use. **Current accounts**, however, are used for spending. They provide an easy way to pay for things without using cash. You cannot get a current account until you are older, but you should know how they work.

When you open a current account, you receive a book of **cheques**. A cheque is a piece of paper on which you write the date, the name of the person or business you are paying, and the amount you are paying. Then you sign your name. People used cheques more often in the past than they do today. Your parents might have used cheques to pay the plumber or electrician. Your grandparents might send you a cheque for your birthday. Cheques can also be used to pay for services such as cable TV.

			£50 Notes		
Date	**bank giro credit**		£20 Notes		
			£10 Notes		
			£5 Notes		
Cashier's stamp	Paid in by				
	Bank of Cornwall Lichfield (309504)	Reference: **100035**			
No. of Chqs/POs	Account **ROBERT SMITH**		Total Cash		
			Total Cheques		
	Sort Code	Account No.	Trans. Code		
	21-03-18	50826791	77	**£**	

100035   21 03 18   50826791

This is a deposit slip, which is used to put money into a currrent account. Deposit slips are usually at the back of a cheque book.

If your current account comes with cheques, you need to remember a few things When you write a cheque, money comes out of your account and it goes into the account of the person or business you write the cheque to.

If you do not have enough money in your account, your cheque will "bounce" and you will have to pay a fee. Therefore, you should know how much money is in your account before you write a cheque. Each time you make a **deposit**, write down the amount and add it to the account **balance**. Each time you pay for something, write down the amount and subtract it from the balance. Cheque books usually come with a **cheque register**, which is a place to record your deposits and payments.

Many people use cheques to pay their monthly **bills**.

Cheques are being used less and less. In the UK, you might not be able to pay for things, such as internet connection, after the year 2018.

What can people use instead of cheques?

When you open a current account, you also receive a **debit card**. A debit card can be used to buy things at shops and restaurants. Instead of writing a cheque, the card is put in the **card reader**. Then you either sign the electronic pad or enter your **personal identification number (PIN)**, which is a password made up of numbers. The money immediately comes out of your account. It is just like paying with cash. You can also use a debit card at to **withdraw** cash from your account from a machine at cash point. Make sure you know your account balance before you use your debit card.

Another way to make payments from your current account is through a **direct debit payment**. Instead of handwriting a cheque, you transfer money electronically over the internet from your account to the company you want to pay. You can set it up so the payments come out automatically on the same day each month. Direct debits are faster and safer than posting a cheque. When you send a cheque, it can get lost along the way.

Just like when you write a cheque, you must record your debit card or direct debit payments In your cheque register so you always know your account balance.

Helpful hint

Do not tell anyone your PIN. If someone gets your debit card and knows your PIN, that person can get into your bank account and steal your money.

Cash machines usually give cash in £10 or £20 notes. Make sure no one can see the numbers you use when you key in your PIN.

What is online banking?

Paying **bills** through **electronic funds transfers** is one example of online banking. Through online banking, you can take care of normal banking activities over the internet from your home computer. You can apply for new accounts, check the **balances** of your current accounts, and transfer money between accounts.

Some banks offer higher **interest rates** if you open a **savings account** online.

Banks use secure Websites to protect your information. You must enter a user name and password to access your account online.

Benefits of online banking

The biggest advantage of online banking is convenience. As long as you have internet access, you can log on to your bank's website at any time of day or night. You can also get up-to-date information on your account balances and activity. This is a good way to make sure no one has stolen your identity and used your money. (You can read more about **identity theft** on page 28.) Another benefit is security. Bank **statements** that are sent in the post can get lost or stolen, along with your account information. This will not happen if you read your statements online.

Are there things you cannot do through online banking?

Unless your employer electronically **deposits** your pay directly into your bank account (usually using the system known as **BACS**), you will still have to go to the bank to deposit cash and **cheques**. Some banks have cash machines you can use to make a deposit, but it is safer to hand your money directly to the person beind the bank counter. After they put the money in your account, this person will give you a receipt.

How do credit cards work?

Credit cards are another form of payment. People use them to buy clothes, food, cinema tickets, and many other things. You have to be 18 to get your own credit card, but you should know how to use them wisely. It is easy to misuse credit cards and end up with a lot of **debt**.

In many ways, credit cards look just like **debit cards**. They are about the same size and are made of plastic. They both have an account number on the front and a magnetic strip on the back. But credit cards and debit cards are not used in the same way. When you buy something with a debit card, the money comes straight out of your **current account**. It is like paying with cash. You must have the money in your account before you can make the purchase.

Just like breakfast cereals, credit cards come in different brands. In the UK, Visa, and MasterCard are two popular brands.

A credit card, however, is not linked to a bank account. A bank gives you a credit card as a way to pay for things using **credit.** Credit is money that you borrow with the promise of paying it back. Every time you use a credit card, you are paying with the bank's money, not yours. At the end of each month, the bank sends you a **statement** telling you what you bought and how much you owe. Then you pay the bank back using money in your current account.

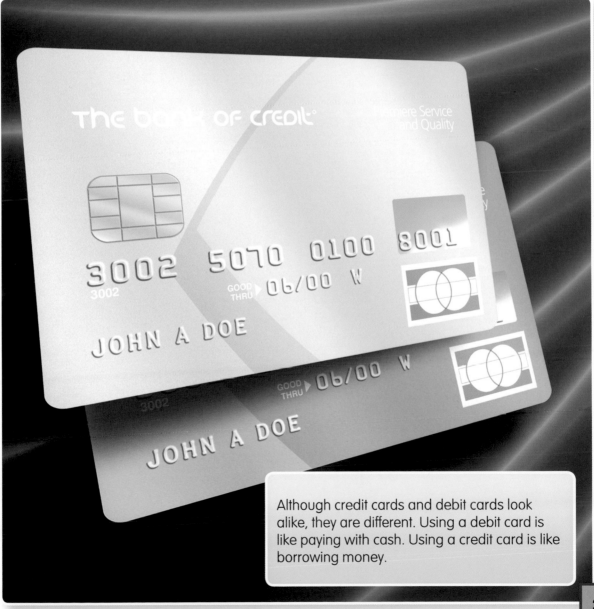

The bank of credit°

Premiere Service and Quality

3002 5070 0100 8001

3002

GOOD THRU ▶ 06/00 W

JOHN A DOE

GOOD THRU ▶ 06/00 W

3002

JOHN A DOE

Although credit cards and debit cards look alike, they are different. Using a debit card is like paying with cash. Using a credit card is like borrowing money.

Dangers of using credit cards

Do you remember how banks make money? They charge a fee, or **interest**, on money that people borrow. The same thing happens with a credit card.

On the monthly statement, the bank lists a "minimum payment due", or the lowest amount you can pay. You can pay this minimum or you can pay more. The bank will charge you interest on whatever you do not pay back, and this **interest rate** is usually very high. The only way to avoid paying interest is to pay back the whole statement **balance** each month.

Each credit card has a limit. It might be £5,000. This means you can charge up to £5,000 on your card. People sometimes have two or three credit cards that are "maxed out", or charged to the limit, and they only pay the minimum each month. This is how people end up having a lot of debt.

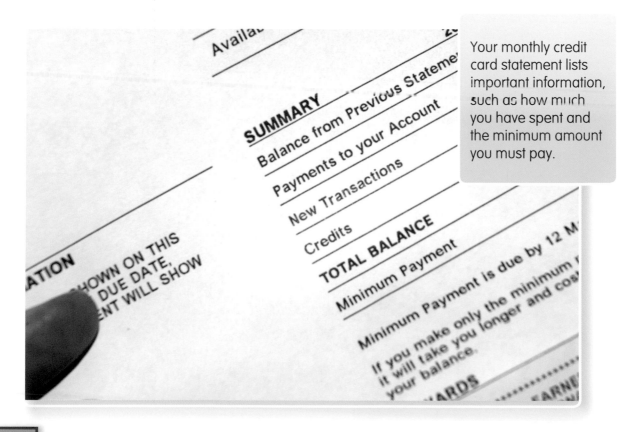

Your monthly credit card statement lists important information, such as how much you have spent and the minimum amount you must pay.

Credit card trouble

Seth is a student who buys a TV and laptop with his first credit card. His balance owed is £1,500. At the end of each month, Seth pays the "minimum amount due" shown on his statement. The bank charges Seth 18 per cent interest on the rest of the balance.

Even if Seth does not charge anything else to this card, it will take him *12 years* to pay off his debt. Seth will pay £1,673.25 in interest. That is more than he paid for the TV and laptop in the first place!

Benefits of using credit cards

Credit cards are convenient. They are easier to carry around than a lot of cash. In some ways, they are safer than other payment options. If you lose cash, it is gone. If you lose a **cheque** or debit card, someone might be able to get into your account and steal your money. If you lose a credit card, however, you can call the bank and cancel your card so no one can make purchases with it.

Credit cards make it easy to shop online from your home computer.

You can use credit cards just about anywhere, for example in restaurants, petrol stations, supermarkets, and many other places. You can also use credit cards to buy things on the internet and to reserve a hotel or rent a car.

If you make your payments on time and do not "max out" your card, you can build good credit rating using a credit card. Having good **credit rating** means you can be trusted to pay back what you borrow. If you have good credit, you are more likely to get a **loan** for something big such as a house, and you might even get lower car insurance rates.

Helpful hint

Only use a credit card to buy something if you will have enough money in your current account to pay for it at the end of the month.

If you do not use credit cards wisely, you will develop bad credit rating. This means you cannot be trusted to pay back what you borrow.

What is identity theft?

Identity theft happens when someone steals personal information about another individual and then pretends to be that person. People steal information such as bank account numbers and National Insurance numbers. While pretending to be another person, the thief might open bank accounts, make charges on a **credit card**, or do illegal things using someone else's name. All of these things can give the victim bad **credit rating** and make it hard for that person to get a **loan**. Even babies have had their identities stolen!

Helpful hints

There are many things you can do to protect your identity:

1. Leave any bank cards at home in a safe place. Don't tell anyone your PIN number or any banking passwords.

2. Ask your parents to get one free credit report for you each year. This report will show if someone has opened a credit card or bank account in your name.

3. Do not open emails from people you do not know. Some of these emails are from people who are trying to get personal information they can use in identity theft. These are called phishing emails because the senders are "fishing" for information.

4. Check with your parents before you give out your phone number or address to anyone, whether in person or online.

Some phishing e-mails look very official. However, real emails from your bank will not ask for personal information, your password or PIN.

Why is a budget important?

Your parents want to buy a new car, but they also need money for their normal expenses, such as food, electricity, petrol and so on. How do they make sure they have enough money to pay for it all? They can use a **budget**. A budget is a plan that lists income, or money earned, and expenses, or money spent. By knowing what they earn and spend, your parents can work out what they need to save in order to buy the car.

A budget is not just for adults. You may not have the same monthly expenses as your parents, but you do get money and spend money. A budget can help you save and stay out of **debt**.

Solve it!

Jenny buys a slice of pizza at school two times per week. Each slice is £2. How much does she spend in a week? In a month? In a year?

£2 x 2 (days per week) = _____ per week

£____ (per week) x 4 (weeks in a month) = _____ per month

£____ (per month) x 12 (months in a year) = _____ per year

Learn to keep track of your income and expenses when you are young.

Write it down!

It helps to find out what you really earn and spend in a month. Get a notebook and pencil. Then write down everything you spend for one month. (See the example below.) Write down everything, whether it is a pack of gum, trading card, or lip gloss. On another sheet of paper, write down your income for a month. Include gifts, pocket money, and extra jobs. Then add up both sheets and see what you get. You will probably be amazed at how much you spend in a month.

Here is an example of how to keep track of what you spend and what you make.

DAY	WHAT I BOUGHT	COST
1	ice cream at school	$1.50
2	candy after school	.50
3	--	--
4	pizza at lunch	$2.50
5	--	--
6	movie	$5.00
7	--	--
keep going to the end of the month		
TOTAL		**$9.50**

WEEK	WHERE MONEY CAME FROM	HOW MUCH
1	allowance, raked grandpa's leaves	$3.00 + $5.00 = $8.00
2	allowance	$3.00
3	allowance	$3.00
4	allowance, washed dad's truck	$3.00 + $10.00 = $13.00
TOTAL		**$27.00**

Wants versus needs

Another part of creating a budget is working out what you need to spend money on and what you want to spend money on. Needs are things like warm clothes or pens for school. Wants are extras, such as crisps or a DVD. When you create a budget, make sure you have money to pay for your needs first.

We all have things we want. Your parents may want to go on holiday. You may want a new scooter. A budget can help you save enough money to pay for things you want. If you know how much money you get and spend each month, you can work out how much money you have left over and how much you still need to save. You can work out if you need to do some extra jobs around the house in order to meet your goal. You can also look at what you are currently spending and decide what you can cut out, at least until you reach your goal.

Solve it!

Reggie really wants a new DS game. His parents say he has to buy it himself. The game costs £25. Reggie has saved £13 so far, and he needs to save £12 more.

Reggie receives £5 a week pocket money. Because Reggie has a budget, he knows that he spends around £3 a week, and he saves the other £2. How many weeks will it take Reggie to save for the game?

What if Reggie started spending only £2 a week, and he saved the other £3? How many weeks would it take him to save for the game?

A budget can help you plan and save for big expenses, such as a laptop.

How do people get money for really big purchases?

Have you ever wondered how people get enough money to buy a house? Most people need to borrow money from a bank in order to make really big purchases. In other words, they get a **loan** from the bank, and they promise to pay it back in a certain amount of time. With a house, this loan is called a **mortgage**. There are special student loans for people who want to go to university. Someone also might need a loan to start a business.

There are two parts to paying back a loan. The person must pay back the borrowed money, which is called the **principal**. In addition, a person must pay **interest** on the principal. Remember, a bank is a business, and it makes money by charging interest.

Solve it!

Jasmine wants to start a business making cup cakes. She borrows £10,000 for five years at 7 per cent interest.

1. How much will Jasmine pay in interest if she takes the whole five years to pay back the loan?

   £10,000 (amount borrowed) x .07 (interest) x 5 (years) = _____

2. How much will Jasmine owe altogether?

Mervyn King

Interest rates for loans are set by the Monetary Policy Committee of the Bank of England, which is the central bank of the United Kingdom. Mervyn King is the current governor of the Bank of England and chairman of the Monetary Policy Committee. King became governor of the Bank of England in 2003. King was reappointed governor in 2008.

What happens when someone cannot pay back a loan?

If you borrow money and cannot pay it back, you **default** on your loan. Defaulting on a loan can cause bad **credit rating**, which means you cannot be trusted to pay back what you borrow. A bank will be less likely to give you a loan next time if you default.

Do you remember what a **budget** is? When you borrow money for really big purchases, make sure you have enough money to make the repayments. Find out if your loan has an interest rate that will increase at some point. If so, make sure you have money in your budget to cover the higher payments when the rate increases.

If a home owner defaults on a mortgage, the bank takes the house. This is called **repossession** (or "foreclosure" in the US). In general, most people do not default on home loans. Since 2005, however, there has been an increase worldwide in the number of repossessions. In the United States alone, there have been over 10 million in that time. The case study on page 37 explains why.

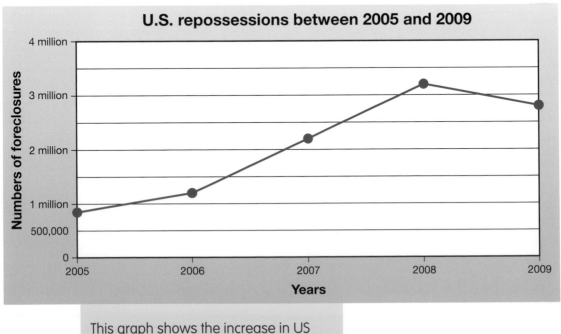

This graph shows the increase in US repossessions between 2005 and 2009.

Repossession

Prior to the 1990s, banks had strict rules about who could borrow money to buy a house. People needed to have a good credit rating, and they needed to make a deposit, or pay some money at the time they got the loan.

However, banks began to make it easier to borrow money. Banks started lending to people with bad credit, and they did not always require a desposit. These were called **subprime mortgages**. Banks also offered very low interest rates for the first year or two. Thousands of people jumped at the chance to own a home, but many did not work out what they would have to pay once the rate increased. For some people, this monthly payment doubled! As a result, many people could not pay their mortgage.

Must be Sold BY AUCTION

In association with Graham Penny Auctions

0207 407 1743

What else can people do with money?

When you get older, you may want to share and invest the money you earn.

Share

Have you ever heard of Oxfam, the RSPCA, or Shelter? These are all **charities**, or organizations that accept gifts of money to provide some kind of help to people in need. You can share some of your money with charities like these and many others. Some charities collect money for cancer research or to provide scholarships for people who cannot pay for their education. Some charities give homeless people a place to stay and help them find a job.

Some people belong to a church, mosque, or synagogue. These are other places where you can share your money.

Charities such as Oxfam accept gifts of money to provide help for people in need.

David Beckham

You probably know David Beckham as a successful football player. Did you know that he is also a philanthropist? A philanthropist is someone who donates time and money to charities. David and his wife, Victoria, have created their own charity called the Victoria and David Beckham Charitable Trust. This charity helps children who are sick or disabled get medical care and equipment they need, such as wheelchairs. Beckham also supports the charity Help for Heroes. This organization helps soldiers when they return from Iraq and Afghanistan.

Invest

An **investment** is anything you buy with the expectation that it will increase in value. Blocks of flats, land, and **stocks and shares** are all types of investments. If you buy any of these things when the price is low and sell them later when the price is high, you make a **profit**.

Some investments, such as gold, are considered safe because the price is more likely to go up. Other investments, such as stocks and shares, are more risky because the price goes down just as easily as it goes up. When you buy **shares**, you buy a small part of a company, or a share in is profits. Your gain or loss depends on the success of the company. If a company does well, its share price goes up. If the company loses sales or has other problems, its share price goes down and you could lose money.

The **stock exchange** is not an actual place that you can go to. It refers to the buying and selling of stocks and shares. In the UK, the **Ftse 100 index** shows the value of 100 most vaulable UK companies.

Dow Jones Industrial Average, 2000-2009

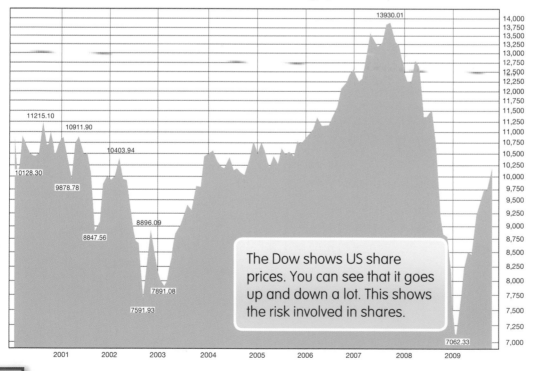

The Dow shows US share prices. You can see that it goes up and down a lot. This shows the risk involved in shares.

Warren Buffett

Warren Buffett is one of the richest people in the world. He is the chairman of Berkshire Hathaway, a company that owns shares in many other companies. Buffett made his money through good investments. Buffett is also a frugal person, which means he spends his money wisely. He has lived in the same house in Nebraska, in the United States, since 1958.

IN FOCUS:

How did the piggy bank get its name?

The first piggy banks were not shaped like little pigs at all. They were actually jars made out of clay. So how did people get the piggy banks that are used today?

During the 1400s, people used an inexpensive orange clay called pygg to make household items such as dishes, pots, and jars. Before there were banks, people saved money at home, and they often used these containers to hold coins. Some people created pygg jars for the purpose of saving coins. Many of these jars had a slot at the top, and the only way to get the money out was to break the jar.

By the 1700s, these pygg jars became known as pig banks and later as piggy banks. Around this time, people started making the banks out of glazed pottery instead of orange clay. No one knows for sure how or when the piggy bank came to resemble the animal.

During the 1400s, the orange clay called "pygg" was probably pronounced "pug". Over time, the pronunciation changed to "pig".

In some European countries today, people give piggy banks as gifts because they believe the pig brings good luck.

Summary

Spending is a part of life. You can learn to spend wisely using a **budget**. A budget can also help you save money.

Age	Jimmy saves £10 a month (£120 a year)	Jimmy's total	Steven saves £20 a month (£240 a year)	Steven's total
8	£120	£125.65	0	0
9	£120	£264.46	0	0
10	£120	£417.81	0	0
11	£120	£587.22	0	0
12	£120	£774.37	0	0
13	£120	£981.11	0	0
14	£120	£1,209.50	0	0
15	£120	£1,461.81	0	0
16	£120	£1,740.53	0	0
17	£120	£2,048.44	0	0
18	£120	£2,388.60	£240	£251.31
19	£120	£2,764.37	£240	£528.93
20	£120	£3,179.50	£240	£835.63
21	£120	£3,638.09	£240	£1,174.44
22	£120	£4,144.71	£240	£1,548.74
23	£120	£4,704.36	£240	£1,962.22
24	£120	£5,322.62	£240	£2,419.00
25	£120	£6,005.63	£240	£2,923.62
26	£120	£6,760.15	£240	£3,481.07
27	£120	**£7,593.68**	£240	**£4,096.89**

The chart on page 44 shows how important it is to start saving when you are young. Over 20 years, Jimmy and Steven **deposit** the same amount of money into their accounts: £2,400. However, Jimmy ends up with a lot more money than Steven because he started saving 10 years earlier. As a result, he earned a lot more **compound interest**. (The **interest rate** in this example is 10 per cent, which is quite high.)

Solve it!

Based on the numbers in the chart on page 44, how much more does Jimmy save at the end of 20 years?

Answers to Solve it!

Page 7

Answer: £10 + £5 + £16 = £31

Page 30

Answer: £4 per week; £16 per month; £192 per year

Page 32

Answer: 6 weeks; 4 weeks

Page 34

Answer: £3,500; £13,500

Page 45

Answer: £7,593.68 − £4,096.89 = £3,496.79

Glossary

adjustable-rate mortgage home loan in which the interest rate changes over time

balance amount of money in a bank account after adding deposits and subtracting payments; total amount owed on a credit card statement

Bankers' Automated Clearing Service (BACS) a UK scheme for electronic processing of payments

barter trade goods and services without using money

bill statement of money owed for goods or services

budget plan that lists money received and money spent

card reader device that "reads" the chip in debit or credit cards

cash point machine electronic banking machine that lets customers withdraw money using a debit card

charity organization that helps the poor, sick, or helpless

cheque written document that tells a bank to pay a person or business a certain amount of money from another person's current account

cheque register place to record deposits, payments, and withdrawals that are made from a current account

compound interest interest that is paid on the original amount deposited plus the interest already earned

compound interest interest that is paid on the original amount deposited plus the interest already earned

credit borrowed money

credit card plastic card used to make purchases with borrowed money

credit rating reputation as a borrower, whether good or bad

currency coins and banknotes used as money in each country

current account bank account used for spending; money in the account is easily accessed by cheque, debit card, or EFT

debit card plastic card used to pay for things out of a current account

debt money owed

default fail to pay back money borrowed

denomination value amount printed on coins or bills

deposit put money into a bank account. Can also refer to money put down in part payment for a large purchase.

direct debit payment automatically deposit money into a bank account without using a cheque or cash

electronic funds transfer (EFT) method of paying bills by electronically transferring money from a person's current account to the company the person wants to pay

Financial Services Compensation Scheme (FSCS) fund that provides money to bank customers if a bank goes out of business. FSCS is not owned by the government.

Ftse 100 Index (pronouced "Footsie") average value of 100 major companies' shares; used to determine how companies in general arc doing in the stock market

identity theft when someone steals personal information from another individual and uses that information to open bank accounts and credit cards and do illegal things in the victim's name

interest fee for borrowing money; earnings on money deposited in a savings account

interest rate percentage owed on money borrowed; percentage earned on money deposited in a savings account

invest spend money on something that is expected to increase in value and earn money

investment anything bought with the expectation that it will increase in value and earn money

loan money lent for a certain amount of time and at a certain interest rate

mortgage loan for a house or property

personal identification number (PIN) password used in connection with a debit card or credit card

principal original amount borrowed in a loan

profit money earned after subtracting expenses; the "extra" someone gets to keep

repossession when a house is taken back by the lender because mortgatge payments have not been made

revenue money earned before subtracting expenses

savings account bank account used for putting money aside for later use

share one "piece" of a company's stock

stateent summary of bank account or credit card activity, usually issued once a month

stock certificate of ownership in a company

stock exchange refers to the buying and selling of stocks; not a real place

subprime mortgage type of home loan given to people with bad credit and/or not enough money for a down payment

withdraw take money out of an account

Find out more

Books

Graphing Money, (Real World Data), Patrick Catel, (Heinemann Library, 2010)

Managing Money (Life Skills), Barbara Hollander, (Heinemann Library, 2009)

Money Doesn't Grow on Trees! A Guide to Personal Finance, Paul Mason, (Wayland, 2010).

Websites

www.bankofengland.co.uk
This website tells you about the function and history of the Bank of England and has links to other relevant websites.

www.moneystuff.co.uk/kids/dictionary.html
This dictionary explains many terms related to money. It also includes a pocket calculator.

Index